Western Girl Coloring Book

MW00955104

____

Test Color Page

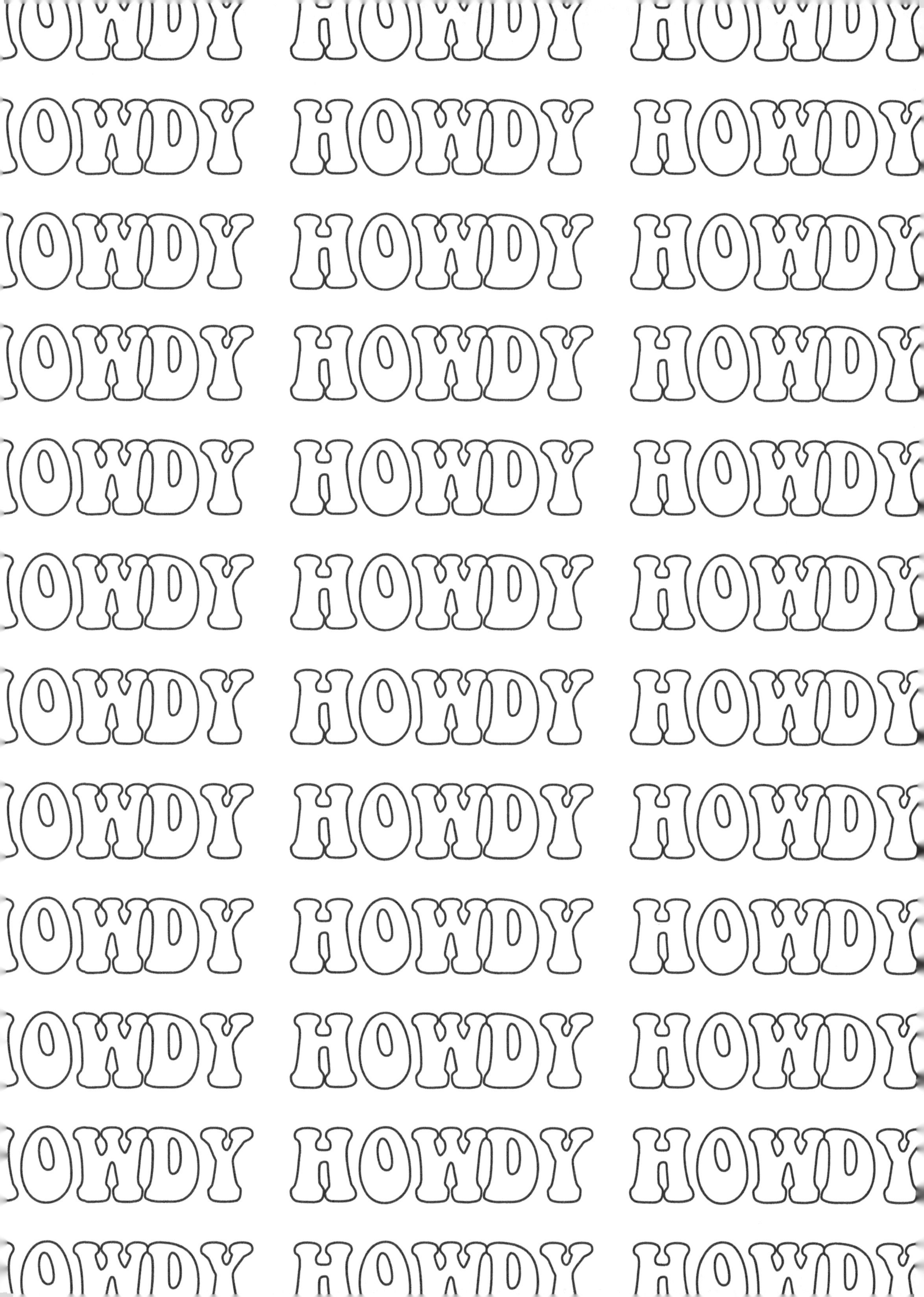
HOWDY

COWBOY
PARTY

IN DOLLY WE TRUST

YEE
HAW

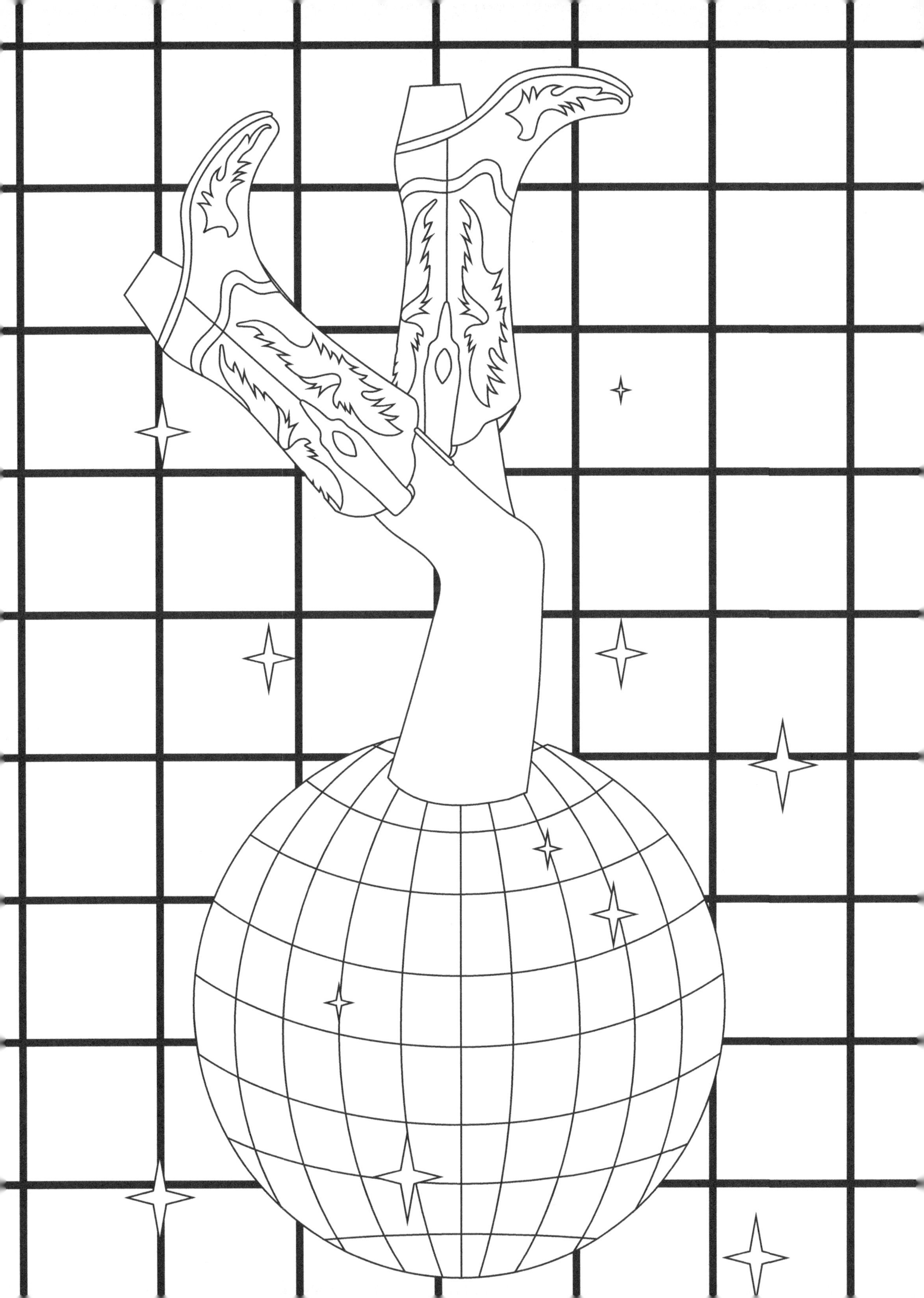

YEE
HAW

COWBOY

PARTY

LET'S GO GIRLS

HAW
YEE
HAW
YEE
HAW
YEE
HAW
YEE

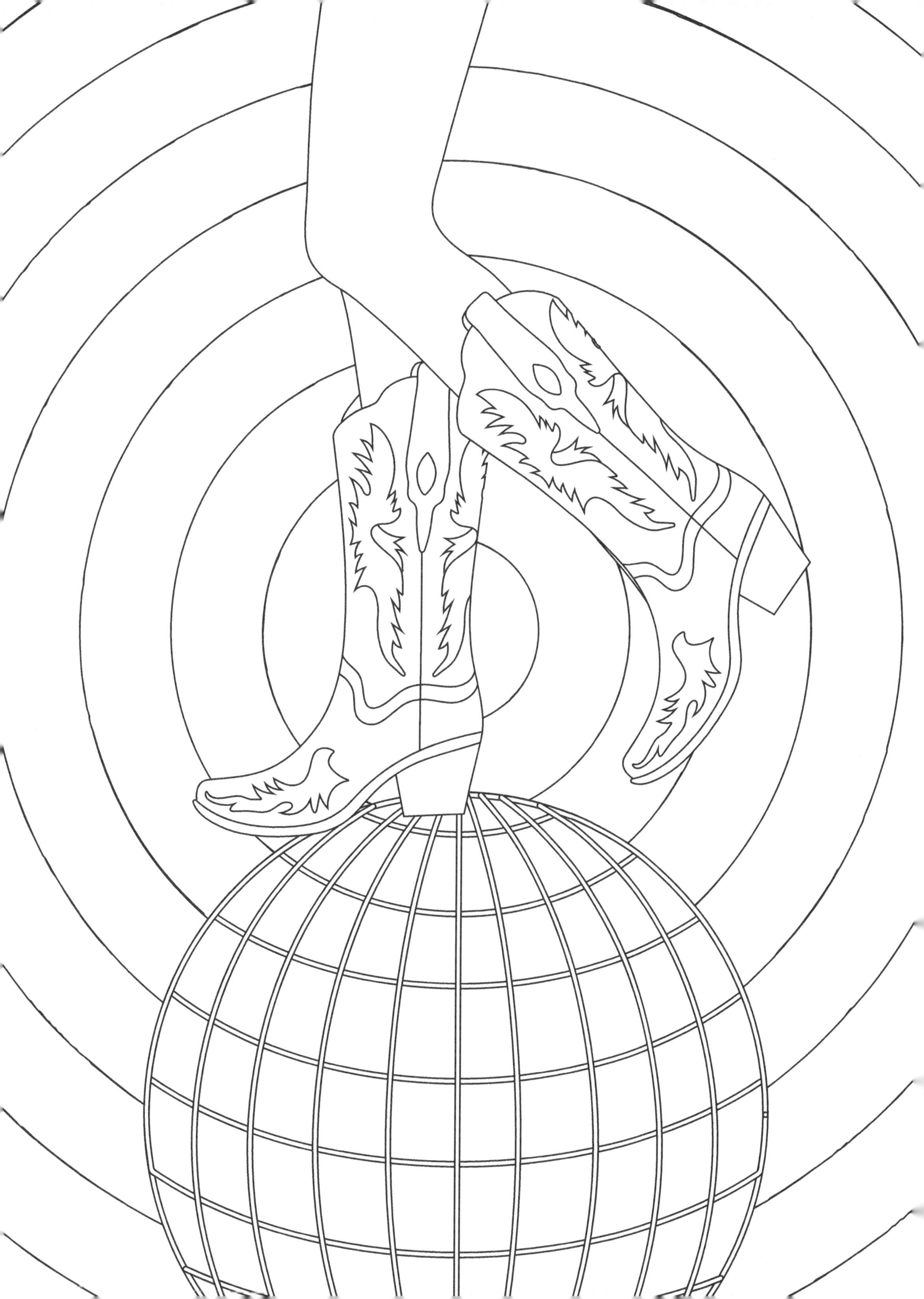

HOWDY
HOWDY

Y'A

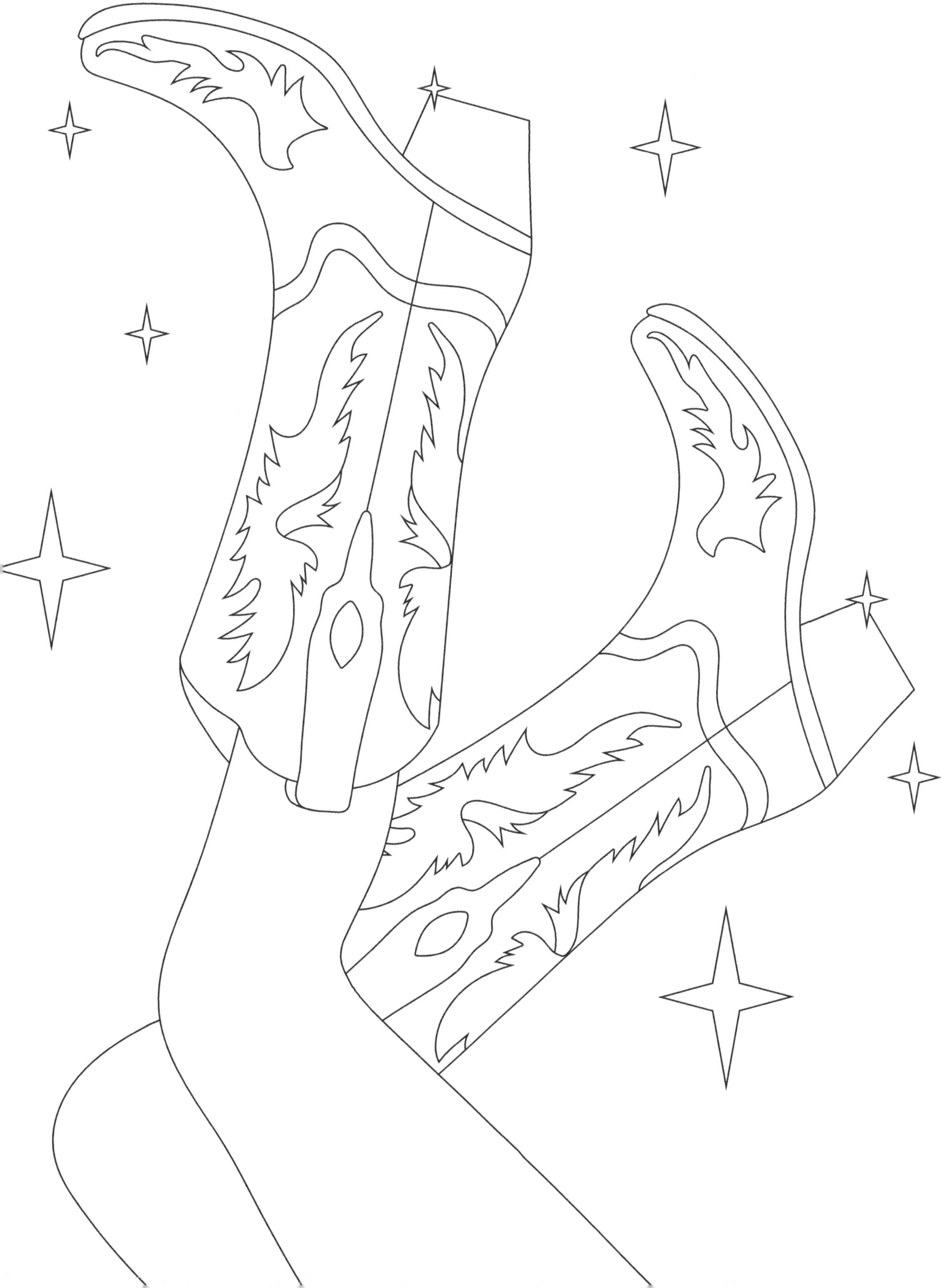

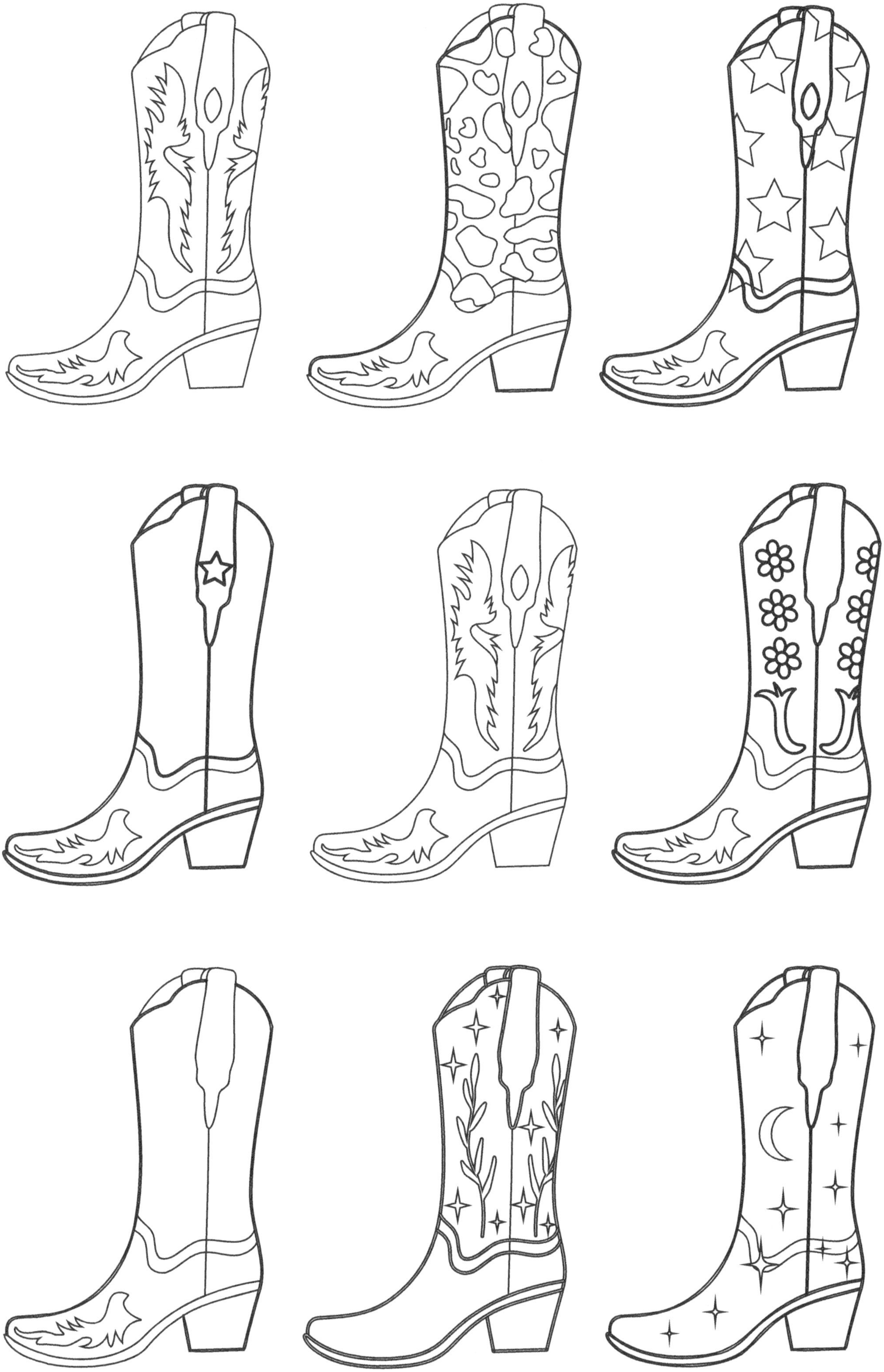

Wild West

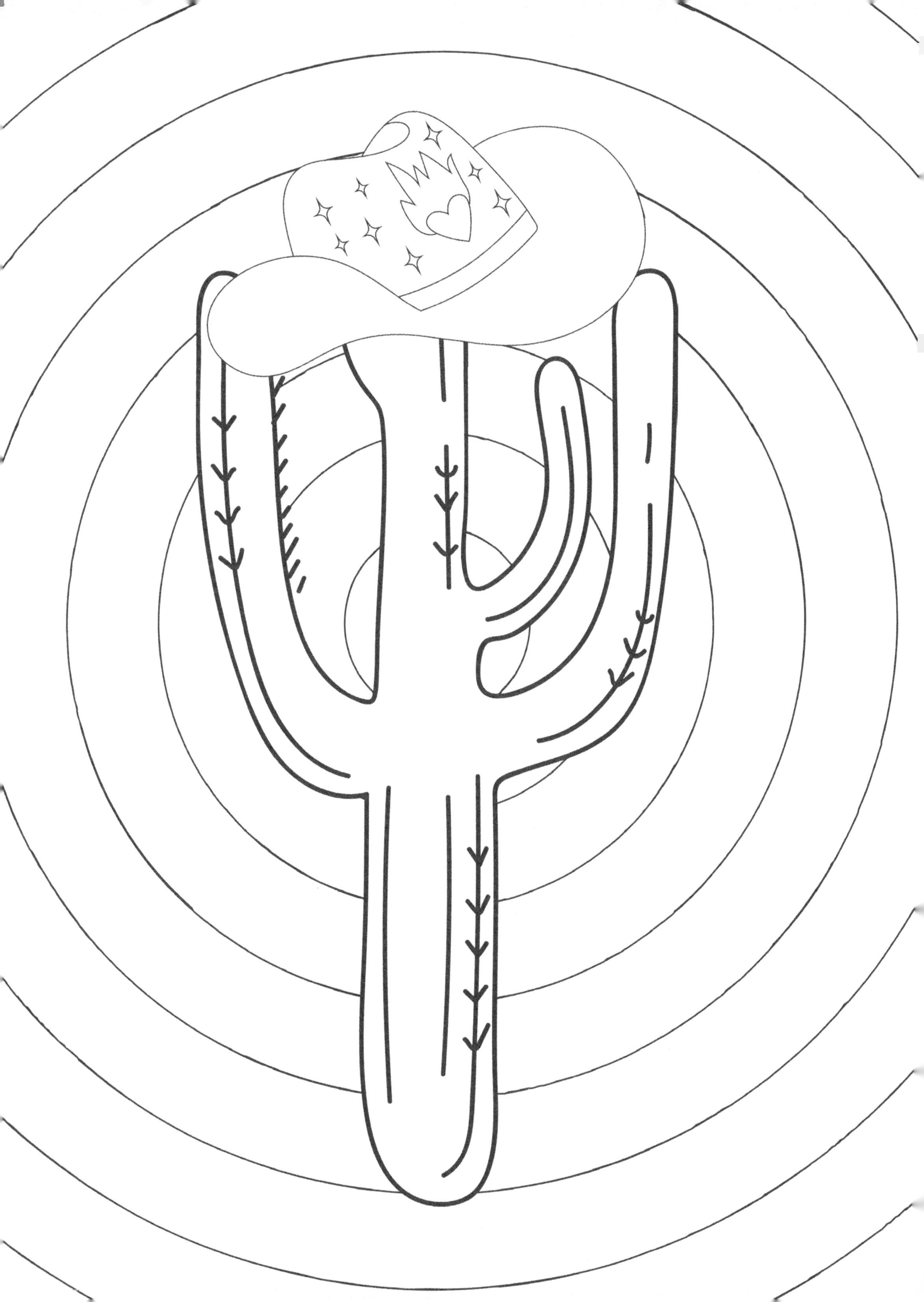

YEE
HAW

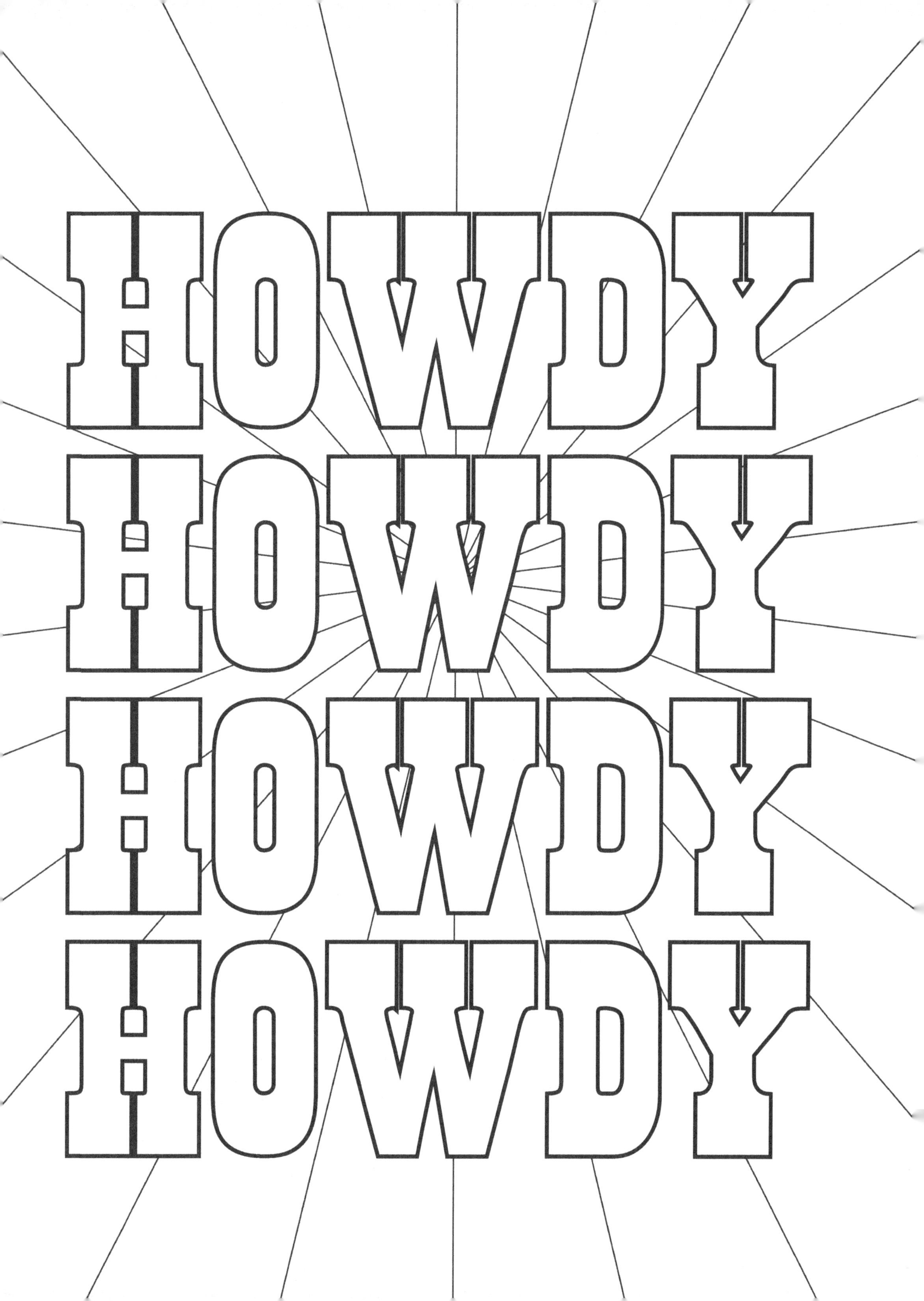
HOWDY
HOWDY
HOWDY
HOWDY

Made in the USA
Las Vegas, NV
25 November 2023

81439558R10024